Contents

	Foreword	4
	Introduction	5
1	Uttlesford	11
2	Braintree	23
3	Colchester and Tendring	35
4	Epping Forest and Harlow	49
5	Brentwood, Basildon and Thurrock	61
6	Chelmsford	71
7	Southend, Maldon, Rochford and Castle Point	79
8	Modern Deposition	95

Foreword

The places in which we live and work have a long past, but one that is not always obvious in the landscape around us. This is a forgotten past. Most of us know little about the people who once lived in our communities fifty years ago, let alone 500, or even 5000 years past. Like us, they lived, played and worked here, in this place, but we know almost nothing of them...

History books tell us about royalty, great lords and important churchmen, but most others are forgotten by time. The only evidence for many of these people is the objects that they left behind; sometimes buried on purpose, but more often lost by chance. Occasionally, through archaeological fieldwork, we can place these objects in a context that allows us to better understand the past, but nowadays excavation is mostly development led, so only takes place when a new building, road or service pipe, is being constructed.

A unique way of understanding the past is through the finds recorded through the Portable Antiquities Scheme of which those chosen here by Ben Paites (Finds Liaison Officer for Essex) are just fifty of 20,000 from Essex on its database (www.finds.org.uk). These finds are all discovered by the public, most by metal-detector users, searching in places archaeologists are unlikely to go or otherwise excavate. As such they provide important clues of underlying archaeology that (once recorded) help archaeologists understand our past – a past of the people, found by the people.

Some of these finds are truly magnificent, others less imposing. Yet, like pieces in a jigsaw puzzle, they are often meaningless alone, but once placed together paint a picture. These finds therefore allow us to understand the story of people who once lived here, in Essex.

Dr Michael Lewis
Head of Portable Antiquities & Treasure
British Museum

Introduction

The Essex countryside is covered in traces of its rich past. From Iron Age forts in Epping Forest to the Red Hills of the Essex coast, there are many archaeological features still present within the landscape. Alongside crops, the fields of Essex produce an array of archaeological objects, dropped by people that once inhabited this land. Thousands of these objects have been recorded with the Portable Antiquities Scheme (PAS) and provide us with deeper insight into the archaeology of the county.

Some of the earliest traces of human activity have been found at Clacton-on-Sea, a site that has revealed a lot about the development of stone tool technology in the Palaeolithic (Early Stone Age). The Clacton spear point is also exceptional, being the oldest known example in Britain.

Farming arrived in Britain during the Neolithic (c. 4000 BC), and so the landscape changed drastically as large amounts of woodland were cleared to make way for farming. As humans moved away from a hunter-gatherer lifestyle, the need to plan for the future led to the development of pottery to store food. With this drastic change in lifestyle came other developments within society, such as religion and the creation of a ruling elite.

With the arrival of metalworking, new tools allowed farming to develop on a larger scale. In the late Bronze Age, tools and weapons were produced in such large quantities that they became more than just practical objects. Large collections of these objects, referred to as

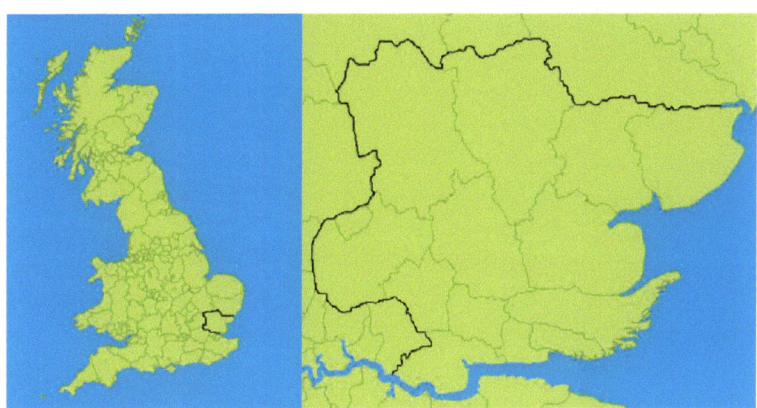

Location map of Essex. (Ben Paites)

A replica of the Clacton spear point from Colchester and Ipswich Museum Service.

'hoards', have been found across the country and seem to have been put into the ground on purpose. Essex has the most Bronze Age hoards of any county recorded on the PAS database. These range in size from two objects to hoards of around eighty individual items. From this, it is clear that Essex was a hotbed of metalworking and ritual deposits in the Bronze Age.

When iron started to be used, society and the economy were revolutionised in Britain. It is believed that this led to an increase in conflict between the different groups living there at the time, as evidenced in the construction of large defensive structures at places like Epping Forest and Shoeburyness. However, there was also a boom in the decorative arts, and many objects have been recovered that would have required great skill to produce (e.g., Find No. 24). At the very end of the Iron Age, Essex was a battleground for the conflict between the Catuvelauni tribe, whose kings were seated at Colchester, and the Trinovantes. This conflict produced some key historical figures, such as Cunobelin (Shakespeare's Cymbeline), and eventually led to the Roman invasion of Britain.

Britain had been in contact with Rome for about a century before Claudius attempted to make the island a province of the Roman Empire in AD 43. Rome never fully had control over Britain, facing resistance and conflict throughout their 400-year rule. However, in the south of Britain, the Roman presence was much more welcome. Within the first few years after the Romans arrived in Britain, Essex saw a major improvement to transport routes and an increase in settlements. As Colchester had been a major seat of power in the Iron Age, it initially became the key Roman settlement in Britain. New sites are regularly being identified thanks to the PAS database, showing the extent of the Roman presence in the county.

When the Roman army withdrew from Britain in AD 410, some remnants of the old Roman regime continued. In the following centuries, even after the arrival of the Anglo-Saxons, it is clear that people often looked back to Rome for inspiration. This can be seen in objects from the period that were inspired by earlier Roman design, clearly seen on the disc brooches pictured on page 7. At the same time, evidence for the rejection of Roman

A comparison of a Roman brooch and Early Medieval brooch with 'sunburst' designs.

Roman (AD100-200)
SUSS-34CFF7

Early Medieval (AD900-1100)
LON-08B190

culture is visible in Essex, with a number of churches from the Early Medieval period containing reused Roman masonry.

With the arrival of the Vikings, Essex returns to the history books. The Battle of Maldon (AD 991) would prove to be a turning point in their conquest of the south. The Vikings were victorious and the first instance of 'Danegeld' payment is recorded as a result of this battle. Surprisingly little evidence for the Vikings in Essex has been recorded with the PAS and the majority of what has been found is in the north of the county. The Vikings did not stay long in the region and it wasn't long before the next major cultural change would occur, after the Norman Conquest in AD 1066.

After William the Conqueror defeated Harold Godwinson, Colchester would once again play host to an invading force. This time, the Normans chose to express their victory through the construction of a castle. This also occurred at several sites across the county, such as Hedingham and Rayleigh. Castles were built both for defence and to show the local people that the Normans were now in charge. Not only did this have a huge impact on material culture and architecture, but also on language. This can be seen in many of the objects found across the county that date to this period (see the ring on page 8).

Colchester Castle museum. (Ben Paites)

Medieval finger ring with French inscription, '*SANZ VOUS NE PA[RT]EZ*' – '*sans vous ne partez/ May you never leave*' (ESS-FD6F87).

The end of Henry VII's reign in AD 1509 marks the start of the Post-Medieval period. Henry VIII, his son, brought about a great deal of change to Britain, not just with the reformation of the church but also through changes to society and culture. After the discovery of the New World, Britain became a major player in the competition for exotic goods. The wealth that came to Britain from the Americas and beyond would encourage the greed of many in power. Throughout the sixteenth century, markets were flooded with the most extravagant objects, some of which have been found in Essex (Find No. 36). However, in the following century there was conflict on a phenomenal scale, in a Civil War that would shake the foundations of the British monarchy and change the institution forever. Traces of this conflict are still scattered across the fields of Essex (see below) and this county was once again witness to some pivotal moments in this significant period of the nation's history.

The size of the county means that each district experienced the events of history in different ways. The objects found and recorded with the PAS reflect the local impact of the many changes that have occurred across the British Isles. This book will take a look at each of these regions and showcase some of the objects that have been found by members of the public and recorded with the PAS, allowing us to learn more about the history of Essex and about the lives of those that lived there.

A Civil War powder flask (ESS-133E3A).

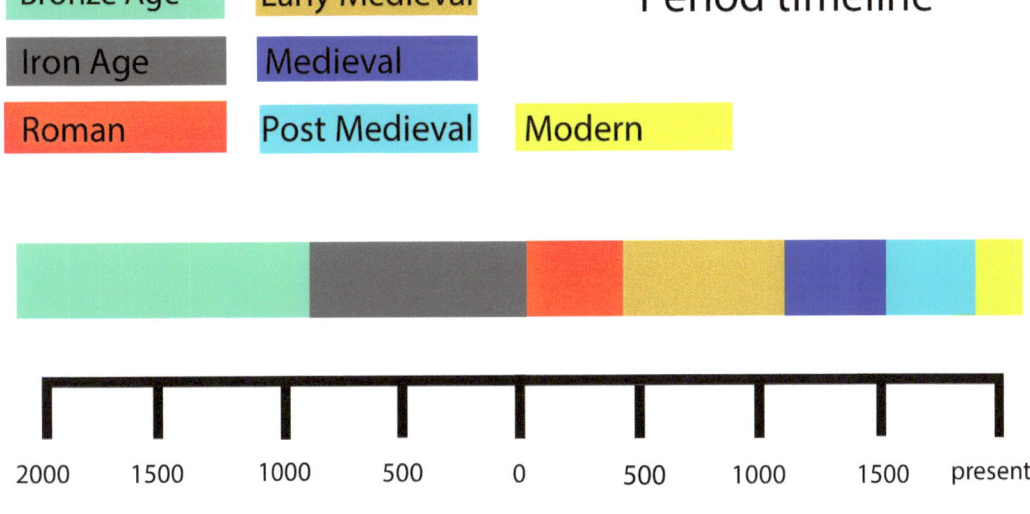

Detecting at the site of the Burnham-on-Crouch hoard. (Portable Antiquities Scheme)

Period timeline

- Bronze Age
- Iron Age
- Roman
- Early Medieval
- Medieval
- Post Medieval
- Modern

2000 1500 1000 500 0 500 1000 1500 present

Years from present

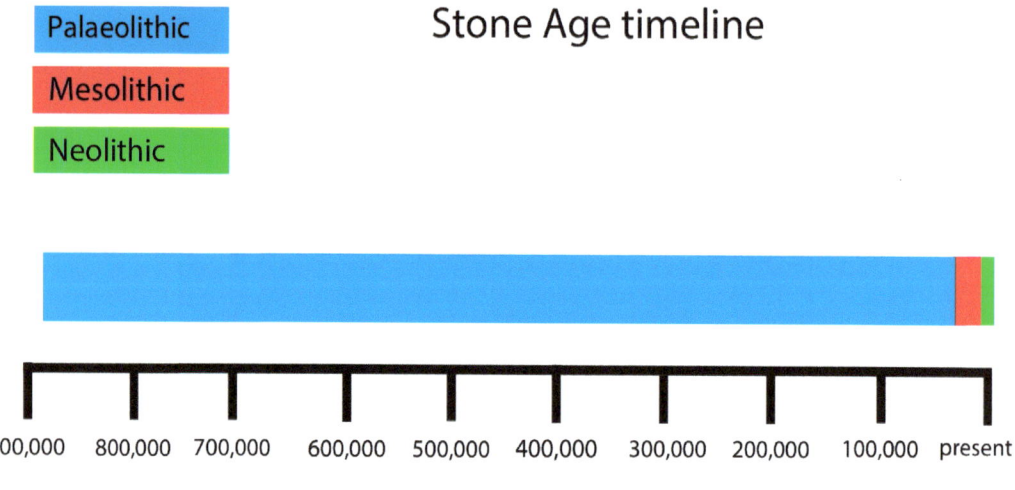

Chapter 1
Uttlesford

Uttlesford district borders Cambridgeshire and Hertfordshire. The administrative town of the district is Saffron Walden, the site of a Norman church and small Roman fort. The wider district was established in the Early Medieval, when it was known as Uttlesford Hundred. This early history is reflected in the wealth of Anglo-Saxon and Viking material that has been found in the region. Excavations have provided some insight into the changes that occurred in this area throughout history, but finds recorded on the PAS database have provided some more personal stories of people that once lived across the region.

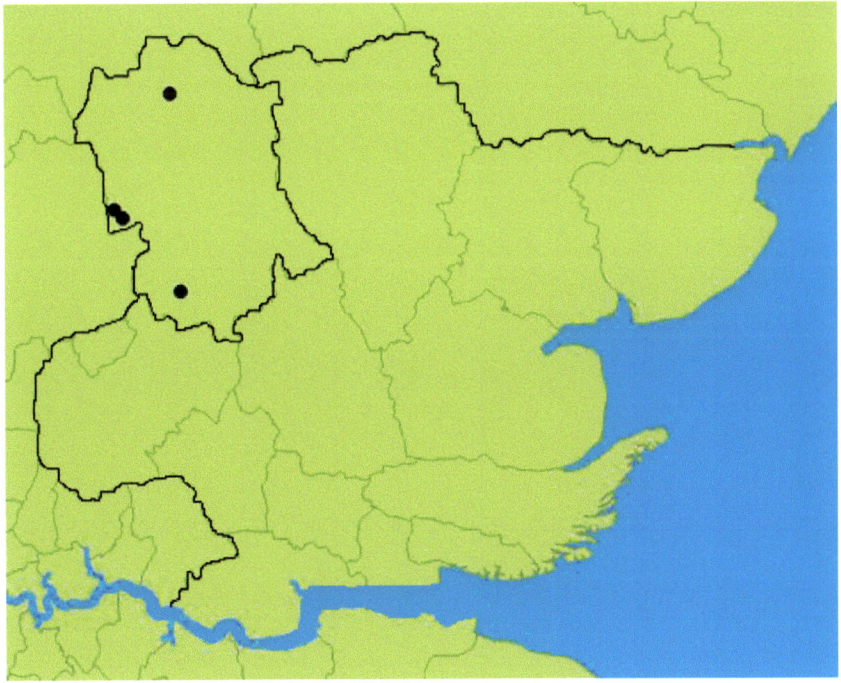

A map of Uttlesford district. (Ben Paites)

1. Bronze Age chisel (ESS-AB4501)
Found near Hatfield Broad Oak.
1500–800 BC

In the Neolithic, stone tools were used to clear woodland in Britain to make way for farm land. When the people of Britain started to make bronze tools, it allowed for more woodland to be cleared, and at a much faster rate. With more trees being cut down, there was more wood to build structures like those seen at Flag Fen and Must Farm. This encouraged the production of tools specifically for woodworking.

This chisel dates to the late Bronze Age, when metalworking had reached its peak. Tools like this would have been vital in the creation of the wooden structures, and their presence in Essex indicates that woodworking was a regular practice outside of the Fens.

Much of Britain would have once been covered in rich woodland. (Ben Paites)

2. Roman figurine of a slave (ESS-6F60D3)
Found in Uttlesford district.
AD 43–410

Recent research looking at isotopes found in teeth and bones from skeletons across Britain that date to the Roman period has shown that people travelled here from Africa, the Near East and even Eastern Europe. These people would have been from a range of social backgrounds, but it is clear from both written and archaeological evidence that the Romans also brought slaves.

This figure of an African slave highlights the attitude people had towards slaves at the time. The boy is not clothed, but smiles and rests his head on his knee as a sign of tiredness. This is clearly what the people of Roman Britain perceived slavery to be, although the truth was often very different. The object is possibly a candle or a steelyard weight. It would have certainly been a domestic item and seen on a regular basis, possibly by a family who owned slaves themselves. It is important to note that Roman slavery did not discriminate by race, and individuals such as the ivory bangle lady from York show that people of African origin living in Roman Britain could have a great deal of wealth.

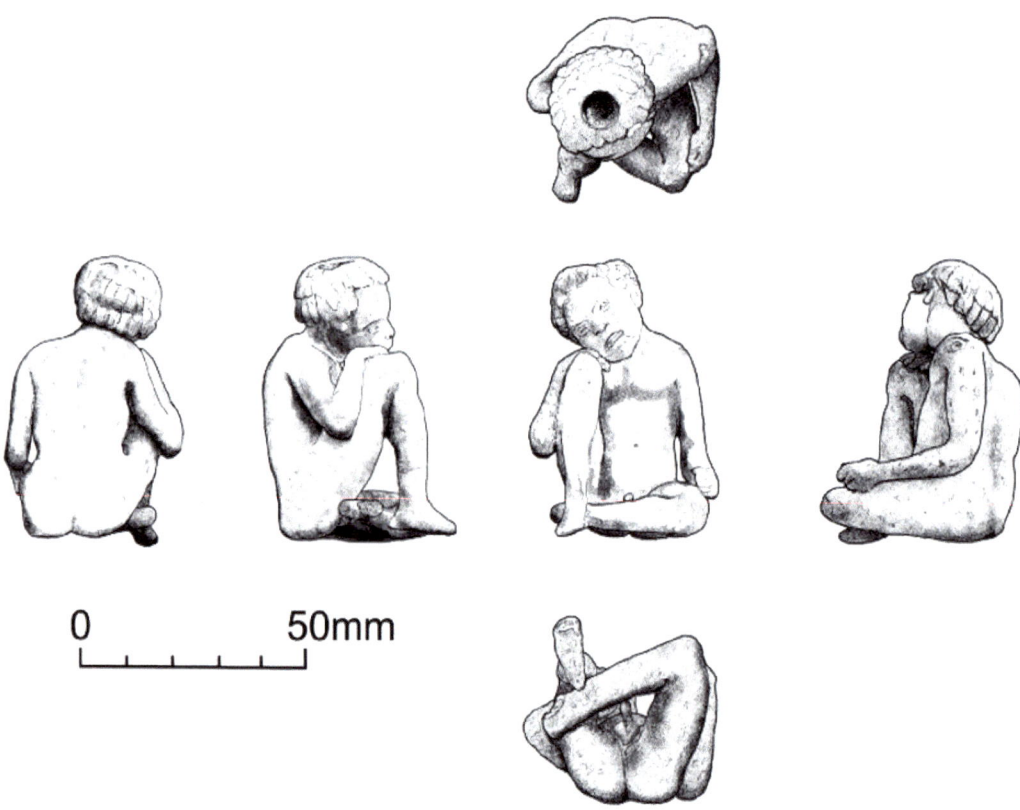

3. Early Medieval pendant (CAM-5BC2F1)
Found in Uttlesford district.
AD 600–700

Anglo-Saxon art is well known for its depiction of a wide range of fantastical beasts, many of which were likely modelled on real animals. The stylised method of decorating metalwork used at the time makes it difficult to identify some of the animals represented on objects from this period.

This pendant shows the incredible craftsmanship of Early Medieval people in this region. The two stylised birds on the front are similar to birds seen on objects from across Anglo-Saxon England, such as Sutton Hoo. Believed to represent eagles, the hooked beaks of these creatures are what sets them apart from some other representations from that time.

An Anglo-Saxon bird mount, found in Bedford (WMID-E4F0C5).

4. Anglo-Saxon finger ring (ESS-E396B1)
Found in North-West Essex.
AD 580–650

In the Anglo-Saxon period, we must draw mainly on texts from continental writers to understand the religion of people living in Britain at the time. When Christianity spread to Britain in the late sixth century, it and the religion of early Anglo-Saxon settlers existed simultaneously for a while. This led to a blending of religious imagery seen on objects from the period.

This finger ring shows a figure holding a cross in their right hand, a very Christian symbol. However, on the shoulder and to the left of the figure are two birds that are believed to be ravens. Although the gender of the individual is unclear, the presence of the ravens suggests that the figure may be Odin. It is likely that the owner or producer of this ring identified Odin as the equivalent to the new Christian god and decided to depict them as the same figure on this object.

Odin with his ravens Huginn and Muninn.
(Ólafur Brynjúlfsson)

5. Medieval mirror case (ESS-0A0415)
Found in Uttlesford district.
AD 1200–1500

Personal beauty has been an important part of daily life throughout much of human history. Grooming is not only important for health and wellbeing, but it also acts as an important social tool to help people express their identity. This often went beyond physical appearance, and can be seen in the objects a person possessed. Mirrors have existed in Britain since the Iron Age, although at that time they were large and were as much a sign of social status as they were a tool for personal grooming. By the Medieval period, more practical mirrors had been developed.

This example of a mirror case shows that the beauty of the object was just as important as the beauty of the person using it. Furthermore, its size meant the owner would have been able to carry it around at all times. A more complete version has been found in Hampshire (HAMP-1F06B3), indicating the extent of the original decoration.

A complete example recorded with the PAS from Hampshire. (HAMP-1F06B3)

6. Medieval bulla of the Hospital of St John of Jerusalem (BH-8F07F3)
Found near Farnham.
AD 1503–1512

Throughout the Medieval period, the Christian church spread far and wide; yet the pope travelled little outside of Rome. It became necessary when administering the edges of the Christian world to issue orders to those in charge of the regions furthest away. They would then spread the word through local communities. These commands often came in the form of papal bulls, named after the lead discs (*bulla*) that were attached to them for authentication. Although most of the paper documents have not survived, many of the lead bulla remain and are regularly found in fields across Britain.

This example is believed to come from Emericus Damboyse, Master of the Hospital of St John of Jerusalem, and dates to sometime between AD 1503 and 1512. The obverse reads, '[+ F.E]MERICVS.DAMBOYSE.MAGISTER', while the reverse reads, '+.hOSPITAL[I] S.IhERUSALEM'.

There were several places connected with the Hospital of St John in Britain during the time this bulla was produced, although it would be difficult to connect it to any one institution. This example was found almost equidistantly from St John's Abbey in Colchester and St John's College in Cambridge, suggesting the seal may have been sent to either one of these institutions before making its way to Uttlesford.

A papal bull of Pope Urban VIII.

Chapter 2
Braintree

Braintree district has a rich history, reflected in the town of Braintree itself. The area of the current town has been settled for almost 4,000 years, with a small Bronze Age settlement in the vicinity. The wide range of objects found over the years in the surrounding fields clearly reflects the diverse people that inhabited the region. Significant sites such as Castle Heddingham also add to the personal histories that we know about from the region. It is not often possible to see individuals reflected in the objects found in the fields of Essex, but there are some examples from this region that offer just that.

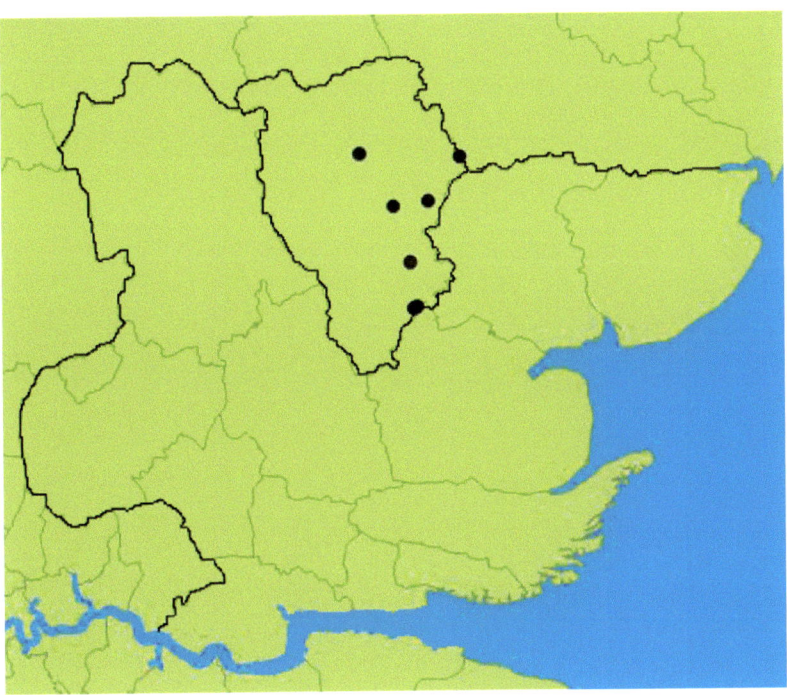

A map of Braintree district. (Ben Paites)

7. Mesolithic flint adze (ESS-35F9E7)
Found near Kelvedon.
8300–2100 BC

The Mesolithic was truly an age of transition in Britain. Not only did the landmass we now think of as the British Isles finally separate from the rest of Europe, but we also saw *Homo sapiens* become the most abundant species. It was at this time that stone-tool technology also began to develop significantly and new types of tool were developed.

One example of this is the adze. Adzes are believed to have been used for woodworking and show the start of modern humans using tools to modify their environment and possibly produce wooden shelters. We have seen how bronze allowed woodland to be cleared at a much quicker rate, but it was thanks to early stone tools like this that modern humans could stand out against the Neanderthals that lived alongside them.

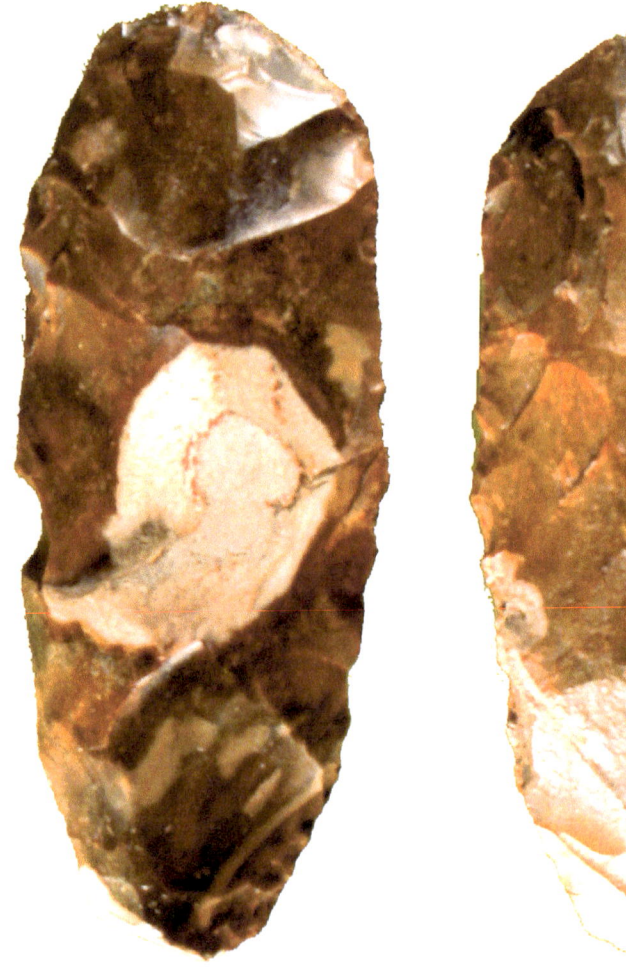

An axe believed to be used by Neanderthal (WAW-7538B2).

8. Bronze Age gold ring (ESS-E97973)
Found near Kelvedon.
1150–750 BC

Gold was used as a status symbol in the late Neolithic and became more commonly used in the Bronze Age as the craft became more refined. Predominantly objects of personal adornment were made from gold, although the skill of goldsmithing increased throughout the period to include more elaborate examples of the craft.

The most common gold objects from this period are penannular rings. They have been interpreted in many ways, but were most likely used in nose piercing, or for hair or bodily ornamentation. The different layers of colour in the decoration of this example are formed by layering different alloys of gold together, showing the level of skill these craftspeople had.

A more common plain gold ring, dating 1150–750 BC (ESS-45C591).

9. Iron Age knife finial in the form of a human head (ESS-B7F8F3)
Found near Greenstead Green.
(50 BC–AD 100)

It is very rare that you get to see the faces of people from prehistory. Thanks to modern forensic techniques, reconstructions mean that it is possible to see some faces using skulls of the ancient people of Britain. However, to see a face produced by someone living at the time is quite special.

This example of a head, probably from the end of a knife, shows how an Iron Age inhabitant of Britain might have looked. The moustache is a common feature on male figures from this period and was likely a fashion observed in real life. Whether this is a particular individual or just a generalised representation of 'Iron Age man', it gives some insight into late Iron Age fashion.

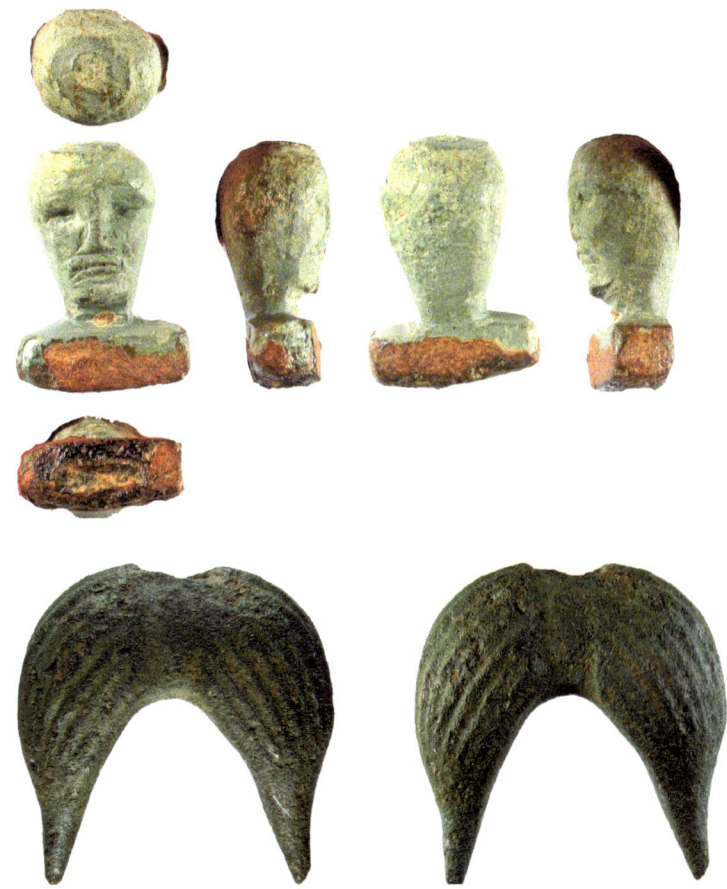

A common but unknown Iron Age object, often referred to as a 'moustache' (WMID-CA9D04).

10. Roman finger ring with a Greek inscription (ESS-455767)
Found near Bures Hamlet.
AD 175–250

We have already seen how far people were able to travel in the Roman Empire. This meant that a cultural melting pot developed, creating objects that expressed characteristics of a variety of different cultures. This was also reflected in the many languages that existed across the Empire, some of which were written on objects at the time.

This finger ring has parallels in many military sites across Britain, although this is the only example with a Greek inscription. The Latin version '*VTERE FELIX*' ('use this happily') was far more common. The phrase '*EYTYXI*' (*Eftichi* – 'be happy/lucky') is has been found on glass or stone intaglios, but this is the only known example engraved directly onto the ring. It likely belonged to a wealthy individual living in Roman Britain who may have had Greek ancestry.

A Roman finger ring with the Latin inscription '*VTERE FELIX*', meaning 'use this happily' (DOR-8F5E8E).

11. Early Medieval scabbard chape (ESS-6DBA05)
Found near Earles Colne.
AD 950–1100

We have already seen some examples of the most elaborate metalwork from the Early Medieval period, but many practical objects were also highly decorative. The skill of the Early Medieval craftsperson was reflected in a wide range of objects, not just those made of precious metal.

This chape would have fitted at the end of a scabbard. It is too small for a sword, so perhaps once housed a dagger or *seax* (hunting knife). It has an openwork design with a plant decoration and an animal face in the centre. Despite the ornate decoration, it would have likely been used on a daily basis and taken into battle or on hunting trips.

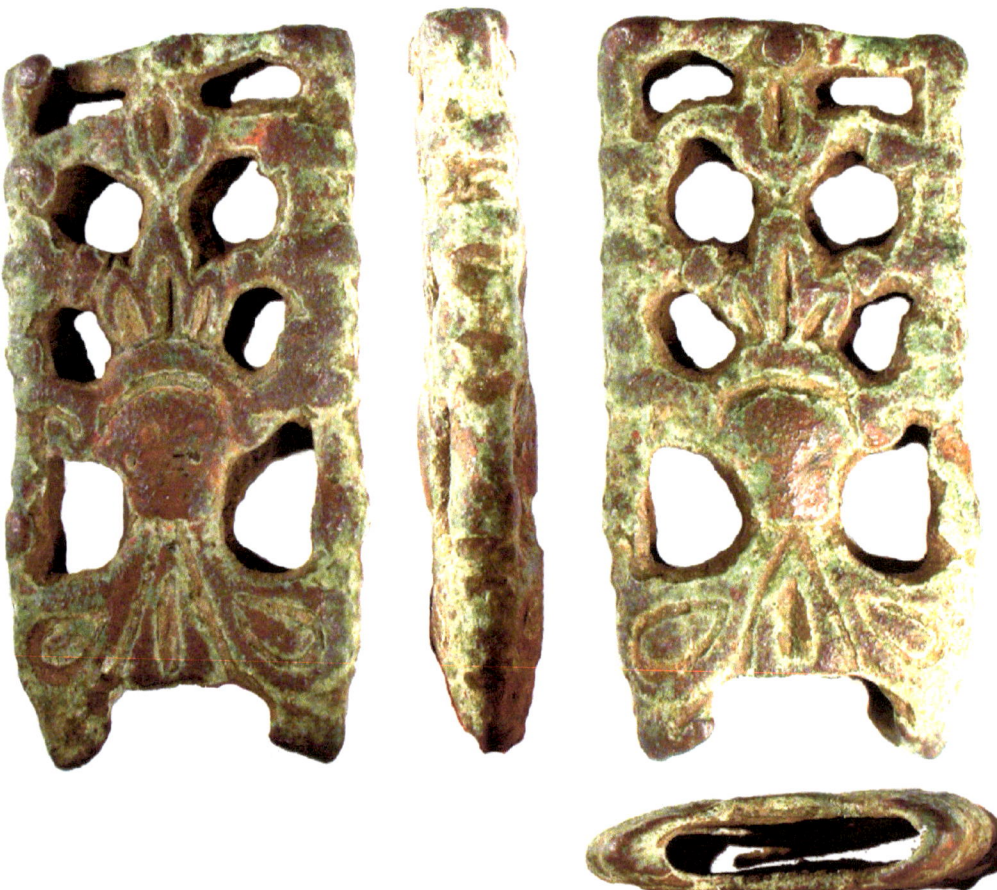

An openwork stirrup-strap mount for Lincolnshire with a similar design (LIN-121803).

12. Medieval pilgrim badge of St Hubert (ESS-940232)
Found near Hedingham Castle.
AD 1450–1525

Throughout the Medieval period, pilgrimage was an important event in the life of any devout Christian. There were thousands of shrines across the Continent to which people would travel. At these shrines it was possible to buy souvenirs, most commonly 'pilgrim badges'. The vast majority of these were made of lead alloy and produced on an almost industrial scale. However, for those who had a bit more money to spend, there were more elaborate examples.

This badge probably depicts St Hubert, based on the presence of a stag to the left of the image. The badge dates to before the Reformation, at which time Castle Hedingham was owned by John de Vere, 14th Earl of Oxford. Hedingham Castle had three large parks, in which the earl regularly hunted. As St Hubert was the patron saint of hunters, his association with John de Vere makes sense. Furthermore, the 15th Earl of Essex, a different John de Vere, had met with Anne of Cleves, whose brother had founded the order of St Hubert in Germany. Perhaps the earl had become a member of the order, and this badge was a mark of that, rather than indicating his pilgrimage to a shrine.

Hedingham Castle. (via www.geograph.org.uk, copyright Paul Farmer)

13. Medieval book fitting in the form of a swan (ESS-19F831)
Found near Coggeshall.
AD 1400–1450

For a long time, books have been more than resources for storing information, acting also as symbols of status and power. In the Medieval period, when literacy was reserved for the elite and religious classes, books were often elaborately decorated and would include fittings that both served a function and acted as decorative features in their own right.

This part of a book clasp is in the form of a long-necked bird, probably a swan. The swan was a symbol of music and poetry in the Medieval world, meaning the book with which this object was associated likely contained poetry or music. It was in the Medieval period where the songs and tales of bards, who had for a long time passed down stories through the oral tradition, began to be written down.

Chapter 3
Colchester and Tendring

Colchester was once the capital of the Roman province of Britain, before becoming a veteran settlement (*colonia*) when the capital moved to London. The settlement was founded in the Iron Age and the wealth of finds from both periods is reflected in the archaeology of the region. Colchester and Tendring make up the north-east region of Essex, with a large stretch of coastland making up much of its geography. However, this region is rich in finds from a wide range of periods. From evidence of early humans at Clacton to the presence of several Medieval monasteries, this region truly reflects the deep history of the county.

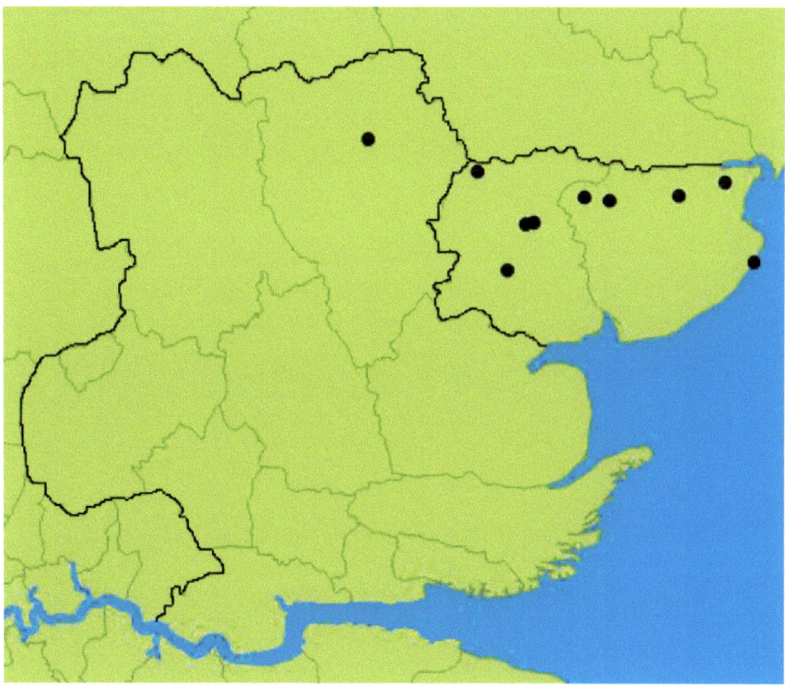

A map of Colchester and Tendring districts. (Ben Paites)

14. Neolithic polished greenstone axe (ESS-43D392)
Found near Walton-on-the-Naze.
4000–2500 BC

Throughout prehistory, stone tool production was an important part of daily life. The ability to make tools out of stone enabled early humans to shape the environment around them and hunt for prey much larger than themselves. However, by the Neolithic period, people had attached a higher level of meaning to these objects.

This axe is made of greenstone, a material not native to Essex. The stone would likely have come from Cornwall, and examples of polished axes made from this material have been found across the country. The fact that it is so widespread suggests that Cornish greenstone was a particularly significant material. The people of Neolithic Britain chose to travel many miles to get this material, before the existence of roads or vehicles that would have aided such a journey.

A replica Neolithic hafted stone axe, from Colchester and Ipswich Museum Service.

15. Iron Age glass bead (ESS-33CCA3)
Found near Ramsey.
800–100 BC

Glassmaking came to Britain during the Iron Age, with the first examples of enamel and glass inlay used to decorate objects. However, the use of glass to produce objects went beyond this, and glass beads became popular among the elite within society. Their origin in the Middle Iron Age suggests a strong connection between Britain and Europe at the time, as the knowledge of glass production likely came to Britain from the Continent.

This bead is an example of a particular style found throughout the south-east, with several examples having been found elsewhere. The swirls were a common feature of Iron Age decoration and they have an almost identical pattern to the other beads of its type. These would have been threaded with metal wire loops and hung around the neck, as demonstrated by an example from London (LON-041951).

An Iron Age bead with copper wire loop still attached, found on the Thames foreshore in London (LON-041951).

16. Iron Age terret ring (ESS-96F773)
Found near Wormingford.
100 BC–AD 100

Humans have used various forms of transportation throughout history, with the earliest wheels being dated to over 4,000 years ago from the Near East. Despite it often being believed that the Romans brought roads to Britain, earlier routes had existed for a long while before. Chariots and similar vehicles existed in Britain well before the Romans arrived and there is evidence of trackways having been present at that time also.

This terret would have been used to guide the reins on a chariot, preventing them from getting twisted together. It shares a decoration with several others found across the county and is quite typical of late Iron Age metalwork. Unfortunately the enamel that would have filled the decoration no longer survives, but it would have originally been a bright red colour.

17. Roman brooch of Bacchus (ESS-691516)
Found near Birch.
AD 100–200

One of the aims of any archaeologist is to identify how old an object is and, if possible, where it originally came from. In many cases it is possible to tell the age of an object by the style of decoration, but identifying where it came from is more difficult. Thanks to improved transport routes created by the Roman army, it became easier for people and objects to move around the Empire.

This particular brooch is believed to have been produced in Roman Gaul at a workshop known as 'Atelier A'. What is interesting about this particular brooch is the imagery. It represents the god Bacchus riding on a leopard. The characteristic spots of Atelier A brooches double up as the leopard's spots. The three-dimensional form is also particularly characteristic of these workshops, although no others have been found quite like it.

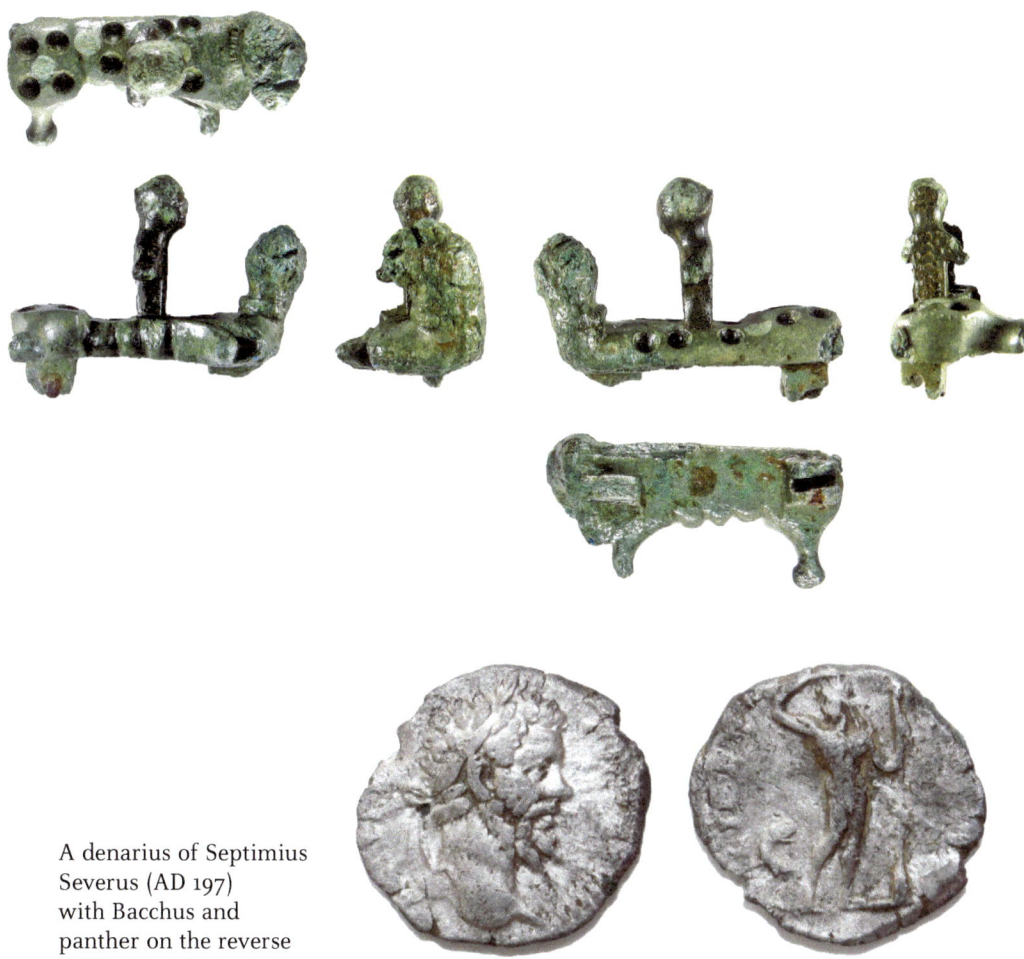

A denarius of Septimius Severus (AD 197) with Bacchus and panther on the reverse (NCL-7C1717).

18. Roman finger ring with Mercury intaglio (ESS-2C0BA6)
Found near Lexden.
AD 200–300

Roman religion permeated every aspect of daily life, and so images of the gods could often be seen on everyday items, as well as in religious contexts. Each household would have had a shrine to the household Gods (*lararium*), at which they would have made offerings on a daily basis. This custom must have arrived in Britain, as *lararia* have been found at villas across the country.

This gold finger ring would have once belonged to a wealthy noble living in Britain. Whether a Roman citizen or a local elite aspiring to a Roman lifestyle, this person clearly appreciated Roman tastes. The intaglio in the ring shows Mercury, the messenger of the Gods, who often symbolised good fortune and financial success. Perhaps the owner was a merchant who wished to win favour with his or her patron deity by wearing this ring on a daily basis. If this is true, it is clear that they were successful due to the quality of the ring alone. Many intaglios depicting gods and goddesses have been found from Roman Britain and recorded with the PAS. Each gives some insight into the personal stories of those who once wore them.

A *lararium* from the House of the Vettii, Pompeii. (Patricio Lorente)

19. The Ardleigh pommel cap (ESS-27D367)
Found near Ardleigh.
AD 575–625

Essex stands out with its range of examples of Early Medieval metalwork. We have seen that decoration on objects from this period shows the high level of skill that goldsmiths had at this time. The designs are matched only by the greatest pieces of goldsmithing in the rest of the country.

The Ardleigh pommel cap is a spectacular example of Anglo-Saxon craft. With similar examples found in the Staffordshire hoard, this object is an example of high status and high-quality goldsmithing. The Staffordshire hoard was discovered within the kingdom of Mercia, but Mercia had not yet gained control of Essex at the time this pommel was produced. The presence of the same style of decoration on an object from Essex as those found in the Staffordshire hoard clearly indicates how the cultural style of ornamentation spread throughout the country. The object was once fitted on the end of a sword and gives some insight into high-status living in the north of Essex during this time.

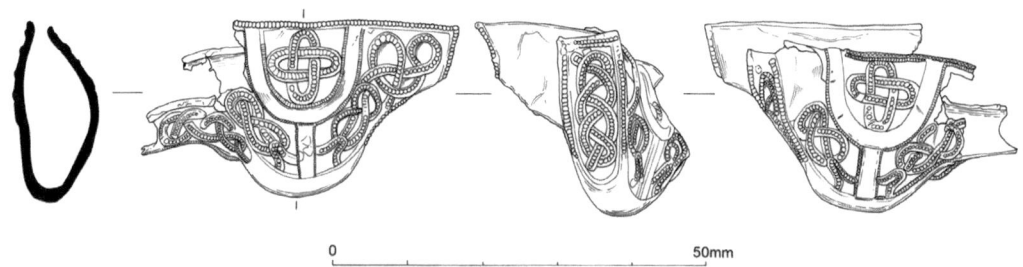

20. Viking sword (ESS-D45534)
Found in the River Colne.
AD 800–900

The Vikings were renowned for their love of warfare; this can be seen in the large array of weapons that were produced in this period. Viking swords were particularly exceptional, due to a technique known as pattern-welding. This meant the blades were more shock absorbent, which was important when in regular combat.

This Viking sword was found in the River Colne, near the modern town of Colchester. Swords were incredibly important to Viking warriors, not only because they were expensive and took a long time to make, but also because they held a great deal of social significance. Therefore, the owner of this sword would not have surrendered it happily, suggesting either that they were killed in battle or that the sword was left as an offering to the gods, remaining in the river for over 1,000 years.

21-22. Statues of St John the Baptist (ESS-49E265 (gold) and ESS-CE7F01 (bronze))
Found near Tendring (gold) and Castle Heddingham (bronze).
AD 1350–1500

During the reformation, many objects that depicted images of saints were destroyed. Henry VIII attempted to revolutionise the church in England, but this lead to the destruction of many significant buildings and objects associated with the church. One of the monasteries to suffer during this period of religious change was St John's Abbey on the edge of Colchester town. The abbey had become home to Benedictine monks soon after the Norman Conquest, not long after the castle in Colchester was constructed.

These two figurines of St John were found in different regions, but both now reside in Colchester Castle Museum. Although it is almost impossible to say for certain, these figurines may have been rescued from the monastery by monks as they fled its destruction in the sixteenth century. It is known that many objects were rescued from the monasteries at this time, but perhaps the monks that attempted to save these objects were not so successful and dropped them during their escape. Having such incredible pieces of craftsmanship survive from this period is incredibly rare, making these two objects vital in our understanding of religion in Medieval England.

Chapter 4
Epping Forest and Harlow

In the south-west corner of the county is Epping Forest. The forest itself is owned by the City of London, but the district spreads much further to the north. Harlow was a Roman town of significant size and an important Iron Age settlement before that. The forest was used from the Medieval period by British kings and queens, with a hunting lodge dating to the reign of Elizabeth I still present. Some of the finds from the region truly highlight the unique nature of the archaeology of the region. Even from fragmentary objects, it has been possible to tell a great deal about life in this part of the county throughout history.

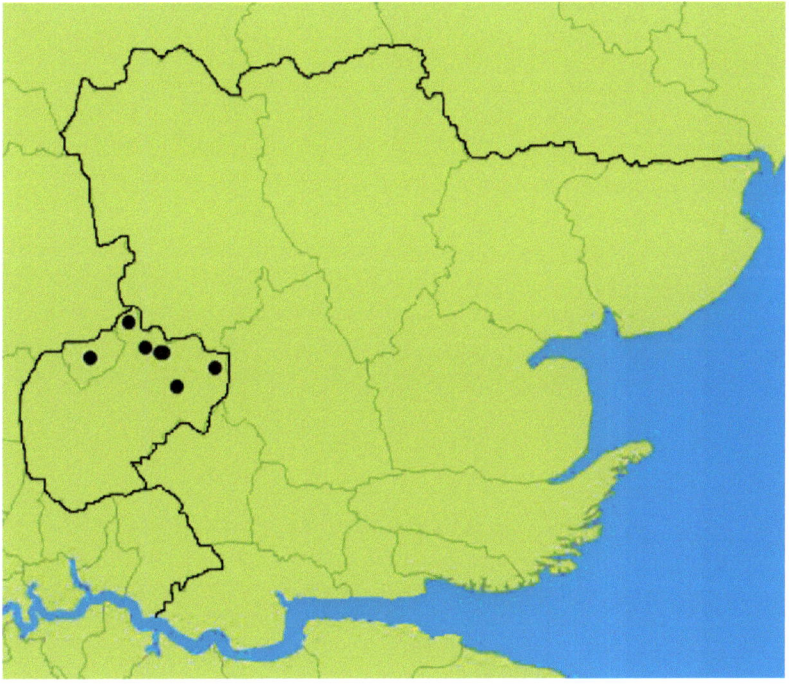

A map of Epping Forest district and Harlow. (Ben Paites)

23. Iron Age terminal (ESS-472ABA)
Found near Little Laver.
100 BC–AD 43

Some of the greatest objects recorded with the PAS are the ones we know least about. It has been mentioned how it is possible to date objects through their style of decoration, but it is not always so easy to figure out what the object was used for.

The decoration of this object is clearly in the style of the later Iron Age, but it is unclear what the entire object would originally have looked like. It would have been attached to another object in some way, possibly with coral or enamel in the rivet hole as decoration. The object may have been part of a handle for a large bronze vessel or even a fragment from a brooch. Although it may be impossible to know for certain what the object is, it remains an incredibly beautiful and important find.

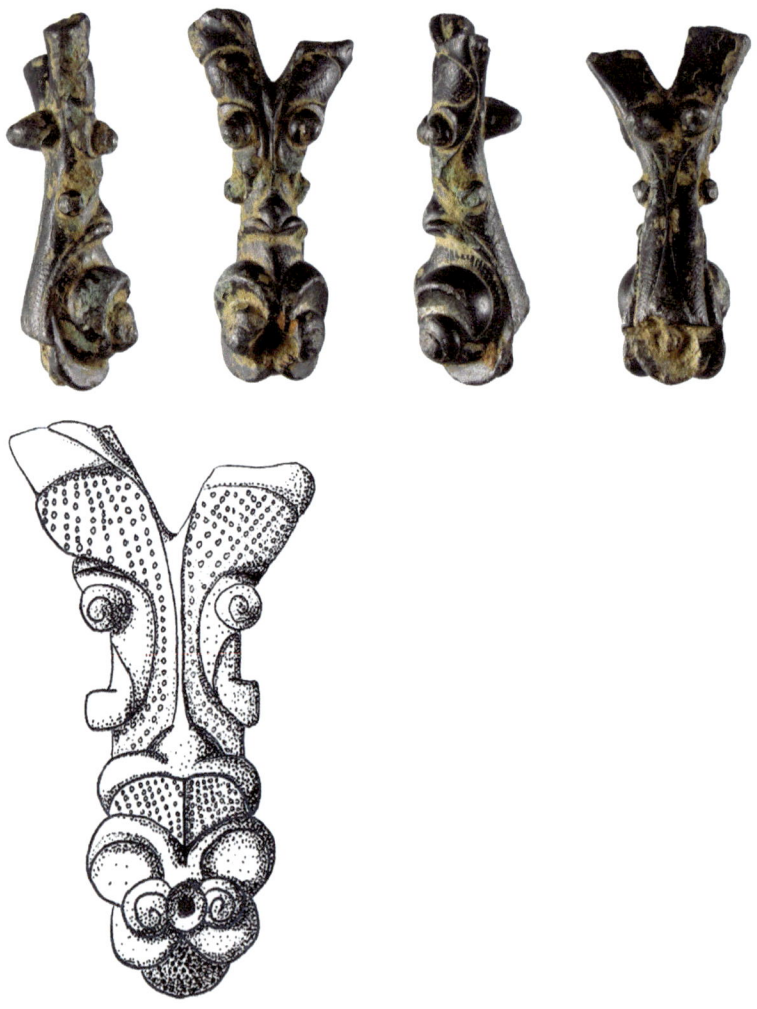

24. An Iron Age potin (ESS-13C8C0)
Found near Matching.
52 BC

Some of the earliest coinage produced in Britain comes in the form of small lead, tin and copper alloy discs called potins. The combination of metals in this way is believed to have been chosen to make them look like silver. Many potins copy the designs used on silver coins on the Continent. Potins were first produced in the 'Celtic' world on the Continent and then began to be produced in Britain in the first century BC.

This particular example is believed to be associated with the Suessiones, a tribe from the Belgic region of north-west Europe. It depicts a boar and wolf locked in combat. It would have come to Britain either through trade or through a member of the Suessiones tribe. It is yet another indicator of how connected Britain was with the Continent during the late Iron Age. Despite the reputation of the Celtic world being divided by warring tribes, it is clear that some cooperation occurred at times.

An Iron Age figurine of a boar, from Wiltshire (WILT-BoADE6).

25. Roman steelyard weight of a woman (LON-E3A604)
Found near Little Laver.
AD 43–410

The people of Iron Age Britain had been trading with the Continent for thousands of years, but it wasn't until the Romans arrived that a standardised system of trade and commerce truly developed. In most instances, this involved standardising the measurement of the weight of goods, so weights were produced to meet those standards. These weights came in a variety of shapes and sizes, with many examples reflecting the society in which they were produced.

This steelyard weight appears to depict a female bust with her hair in a bun. It has been suggested that this represents Juno Moneta, goddess of funds, often seen on coins in the third century. The steelyard balance was formed of a long arm hung from a central pivot, with a weight at one end and the thing being weighed hung from a hook at the other end. The possible connection with Moneta may indicate a connection with coins.

A Republican *denarius*, showing Juno Moneta on the obverse (HAMP3395).

A Roman steelyard with weight attached. (Wellcome images)

26. Early Medieval brooch (ESS-1ACFC9)
Found near Fyfield.
AD 900–1100

The use of enamel in the decoration of brooches existed since the Iron Age, although the way it was used changed throughout history. In the Early Medieval period, strips of metal were soldered onto the object to create shapes, and then fragments of glass were placed into them. This meant that most decoration was often in the form of geometric designs.

Several examples similar to this brooch have been found in the Epping Forest area. All have similar but distinct designs, formed using the same technique. As mentioned previously, many examples are very similar in design to late Roman brooches.

Other common designs found on brooches at the time (left to right: ESS-0A8B65, LON-5E4038 and ESS-BD2421).

27. Early Medieval gold pin head (ESS-3ECB42)
Found near Harlow.
AD 700–1200

The skill of the goldsmith continued from the Anglo-Saxon into the Medieval period, where the design of many objects was very similar to those produced in the earlier period. This has made it difficult for some objects to be accurately dated, especially if the function of the object is uncertain.

This trapezoidal object was probably from the head of a dress pin, used to hold together thick woollen clothing. It is hard to say for certain whether this would have been worn by a man or woman, although evidence suggests that it was women more often who wore such items. The shape is similar to that of a stylus eraser, but it is not certain whether this had any connection to the wearer. During the Early Medieval period and into the Later Medieval period, writing was exclusively an activity of the nobility and the church. It is well documented that women lived and worked in monasteries during this period, so perhaps this would have belonged to such a person.

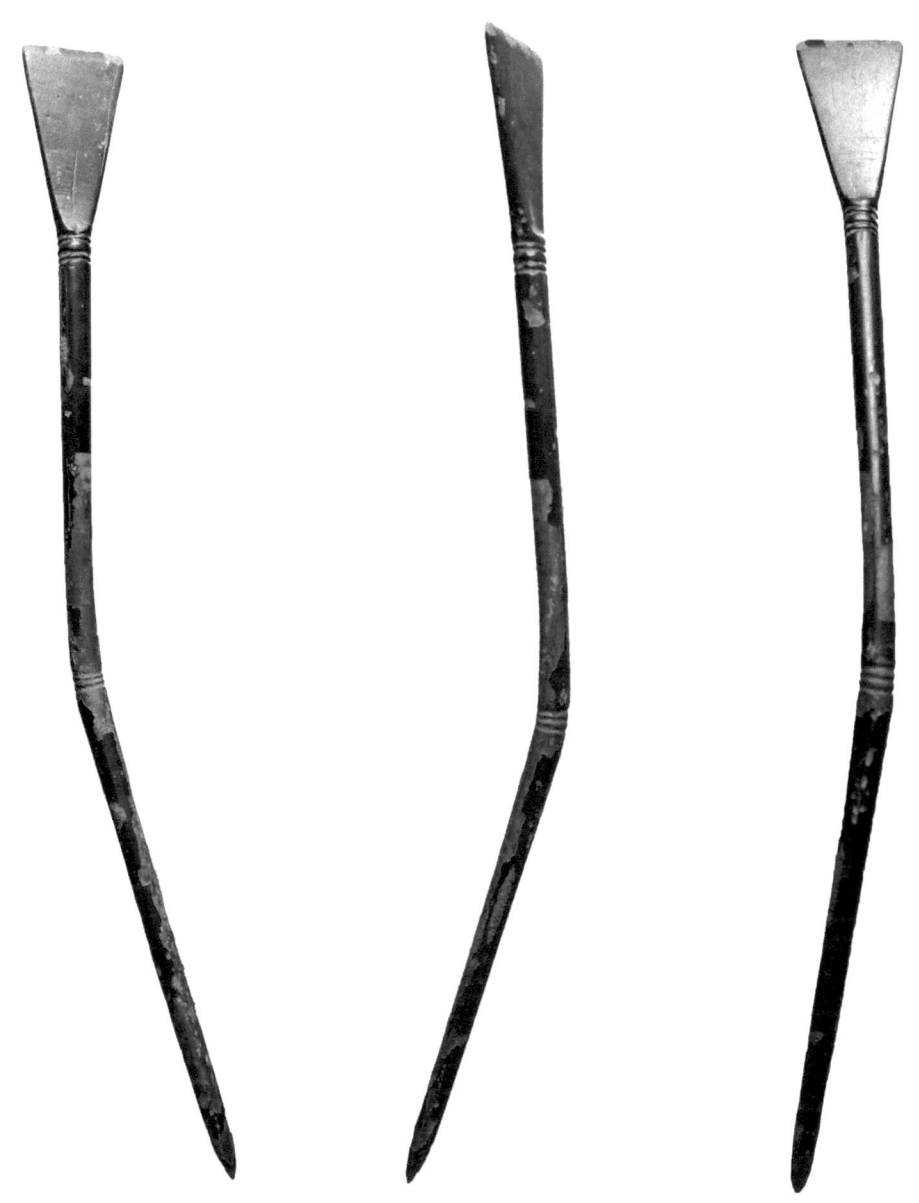

An Early Medieval stylus from Lincolnshire (LIN-F3576C).

28. Mount from a Medieval casket (ESS-13DCF4)
Found near Willingale.
AD 1100–1200

Before the Reformation, objects associated with the church were often highly decorative and expressed the height of decadence in the Medieval period. The most elaborate objects were those associated with holy items, such as the Eucharist or sacred relics. Boxes containing these objects were covered in beautiful ornamentation.

This object would likely have been mounted onto the side of such a box and would have contained a cabochon (a bright, coloured dome-shaped stone) in the oval recess. Its discovery in the middle of a field in Essex is truly intriguing, as there are no known religious settlements surrounding its findspot. However, as with some of the other pre-Reformation items we have already seen, it is possible this object was dropped as monks or nuns fled persecution in the early sixteenth century.

29. Seal matrix of Henry, son of Henry of Essex (ESS-9419A5)
Found near Sheering.
AD 1100–1200.

In the Medieval period, the sealing of documents was a regular occurrence. Any legal document had to be authenticated by the correct authority, due to the complexity of the feudal power system in place. Individuals at different levels of the system could pass judgement on certain things, meaning the seal of authentication ensured the change could take place.

Seal matrices like this one were used to authorise documentation, and so had the name of the official written on them. This seal belonged to Henry, son of Henry of Essex. There is a Henry of Essex who was constable of England during the reigns of Stephen (AD 1135–1154) and Henry II (AD 1154–1189). More importantly, Henry owned Rayleigh Castle in south Essex throughout his time in power. The estimated date of the seal itself make it likely the seal belonged to one of his sons.

Chapter 5
Brentwood, Basildon and Thurrock

In southern Essex, the districts of Brentwood, Basildon and Thurrock border the river Thames and would have seen many travellers stopping there throughout their history. Home to the second cathedral in the county at Brentwood, the site of a significant Anglo-Saxon town at Mucking and grazing site for mammoths in the Palaeolithic, this part of the county has seen a great deal of human history.

The wealth that would have passed through the region from ships returning from across the world is clearly reflected in the historical records. It is also seen in the objects that have been found. Not only do the finds reflect Britain's international connection throughout time, but also the wealth that was accumulated through its contact with the wider world.

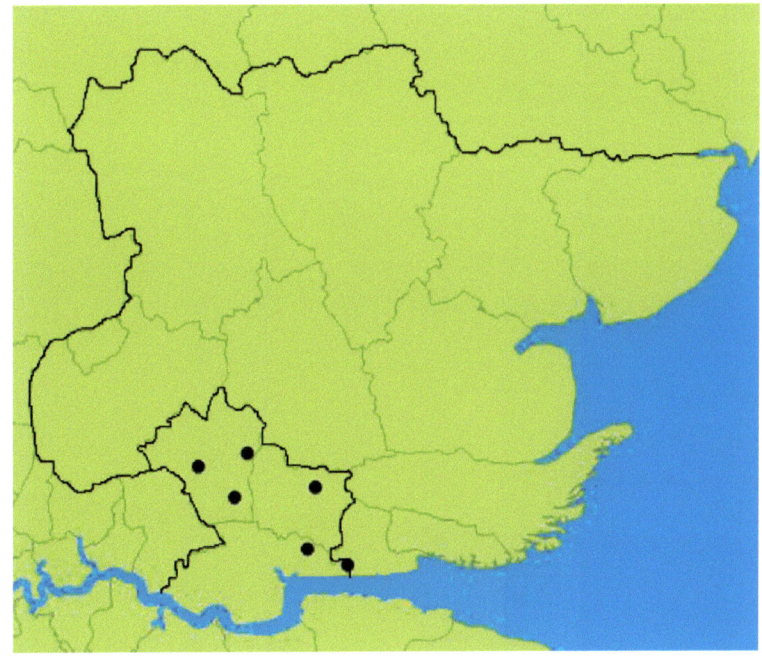

A map of Brentwood and Basildon districts and Thurrock Unitary Authority. (Ben Paites)

30. Early Medieval coin pendant (ESS-10F463)
Found near Billericay.
AD 491–600

In the Early Medieval period, there is a lot of evidence for the reuse of objects from the Roman occupation. It is known that some settlements from the Roman period were inhabited after the arrival of the Anglo-Saxons. Similarly, Rome continued to have some presence in Europe after its defeat at the hands of numerous tribes across the continent. Thus, despite Britain no longer being a Roman province, the presence of Rome was felt long after the army withdrew.

This coin is a copy of a solidus of Anastasius, produced in the sixth century AD. What is interesting is that the coin was used as a pendant rather than as currency. Many similar coins that were converted into pendants have been found across Essex. Perhaps the wearer appreciated the beauty of these objects and had a connection to the Roman Empire, or perhaps these were worn as a sign of defiance against the once-powerful Romans. In either case, it is clear that taking such high-value coins out of circulation was an especially important thing.

31. Hinged mount depicting Jesus Christ (ESS-E41FE8)
Found near Crays Hill.
AD 1300–1400

Much as in Roman Britain, during the Medieval period religion permeated daily life. There are many ways in which Christianity was expressed through personal possessions, from the use of crosses to symbols of the Holy Trinity. These symbols were used to express the wearer's religious devotion, demonstrating it to anyone they encountered.

The image on this object is believed to be Jesus Christ. Objects referring to Christ at this time more often had the monogram *IhS* (*Ih[esu]s*), referring to Jesus, rather than featuring an image. The object is probably from the cover of a locket and is dated to the fourteenth century AD. The function of these lockets in the medieval world is not very well understood. However, some of the examples that have religious and iconographic imagery may have often contained a piece of sacred material. In this instance, it is possible that the locket held a fragment of an object associated with Christ himself. Likely candidates include a piece of the cross or the spear that pierced Christ's side. In any case, it is an example of fine medieval metalwork and a beautiful object in its own right.

A medieval hooked tag with '*ihs*' inscribed on the front (ESS-B84B61).

32. Medieval silver coin from India (ESS-E70306)
Found west of Canvey Island.
AD 1325–1351

Contact between Asia and Europe had existed for centuries by the Medieval period. This connection was enhanced through the exchange of goods along the Silk Road. In rare instances, coins from far away countries would also make their way into Europe and many have been found across the country.

This coin was issued for Muhammad III bin Tughluq in India, at some point between the years AD 1325 and 1351. It was possibly brought to England by boat and dropped overboard or lost when a ship wrecked off the coast on the way to or from London. Two ships are known to have been wrecked near this location at that date: the *Constance* in AD 1343 and an unknown ship in AD 1345. We cannot say for certain whether this coin came from either of them, but it is a likely explanation for where the coins were found.

33. The Corringham hoard, deposited (ESS-AB0B30)
Found near Corringham.
c. AD 1342

Medieval coin hoards have been found across Britain, with several coming from Essex. The term 'hoard' often conjures up a certain image that includes a large quantity of coins within a vessel of some kind. In many instances, however, the container does not survive and a hoard of coins is simply identified as a large quantity being found in a single area.

The Corringham hoard is a rare case in which the container was found alongside the contents. The hoard consisted of 519 Medieval coins, dating from the reign of Edward I (*c.* AD 1279) to the reign of Edward III (*c.* AD 1377). The reason why someone in the late fourteenth century chose to deposit these coins in a container in the middle of a field in England is unknown. Many people have speculated why coin hoards occur, suggesting that people would have deposited coins during times of conflict. This is not always correct and it is just as likely that the coins were buried as a form of savings account.

A penny of Edward I, not from the hoard (BH-BE772F).

A penny of Edward III, not from the hoard (ESS-CF7E56).

34. Medieval heraldic pendant (ESS-DEC2A7)
Found near South Weald.
AD 1300–1400

As society became more and more stratified in medieval England, the nobility used images to tell the difference between the many noble households that were established. Those images became part of the crests of the noble families and were used by their descendants to claim their ancestry. Animals were often used within these crests, although medieval depictions of animals tended to be quite stylistic and consequently it isn't always easy to identify the animal that was meant to be depicted.

The object below is a pendant that would have hung on a horse's harness. The animal appears to be a lion passant, although it was originally interpreted as a monkey. The colour is formed from enamel and would have been unique to its owner, in order to separate it from other nobles that used monkeys or lions in their heraldry.

A mount in the form of a Lion passant (SWYOR-DB1BA5).

35. Elizabethan pendant (ESS-0144A4)
Found in south-west Essex.
AD 1550–1650

The discovery of the New World and the expansion of English trade networks in the sixteenth century meant that precious metal and stones came flooding into the markets of Europe. This allowed for an explosion in jewellery production and, among the upper levels of society, clothing became encrusted with jewels.

This example of a pendant, made of gold and containing diamond and ruby settings, would have been produced in the latter half of the sixteenth century. It would have probably hung from a ribbon or bow, with a pearl hanging from the loop at the base. A similar example has been identified in the Armada portrait of Elizabeth I. Perhaps lost during a journey through the Essex countryside, it would have been sorely missed by its owner.

Chapter 6
Chelmsford

Nestled in the heart of Essex is the county town of Chelmsford. It was the second-largest Roman town in Essex and a major site in the Roman period. The town that stands today was founded after the Norman Conquest; it became a major market. Its development into a trading hub made it the natural choice for the capital of the county.

The town and district's history stretches much further back than the Roman period. There is evidence of an human presence in the area as early as the Palaeolithic. The region was important in the medieval period, with Writtle playing host to several monarchs. Despite less evidence from some periods, it would seem that the region remained important throughout much of human history.

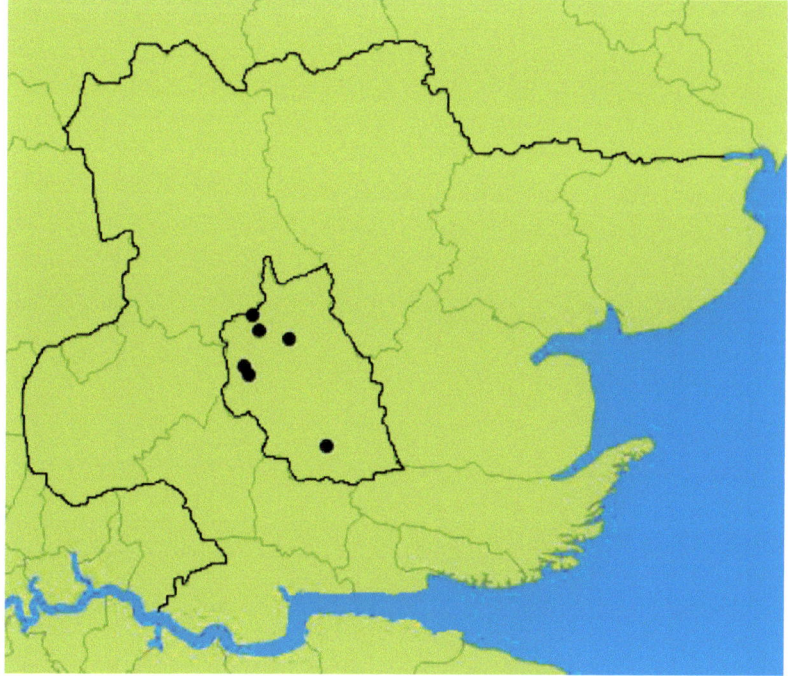

A map of Chelmsford district. (Ben Paites)

36. Palaeolithic hand axe (ESS-445918)
Found near Broomfield.
500,000–10,000 BC

One of the oldest objects recorded in Essex is this hand axe, dated to the lower Palaeolithic. Hand axes such as these belong to the Acheulian tool industry, which is believed to have first been used by *Homo habilis*, one of the earliest species of human. By the time the technology came to Britain, it was likely used by *Homo heidelbergensis*. These early humans lived and hunted in Britain from as early as 600,000 years ago until around 140,000 years ago, when all species of human appear to have disappeared from Britain. These hand axes were used for butchery, and it is believed that the early humans would chase large prey, such as elephants and rhinoceroses, off of cliffs to kill them before cutting them up for food.

37. Iron Age strap slide (ESS-049E64)
Found near Mashbury.
150 BC–AD 100

Throughout the Late Iron Age the *triskele* (three-pronged swirl) was used to decorate a wide range of objects. Used again in the Early Medieval period, it has often been seen as a sign of Celtic identity. The meaning behind the *triskele* has long since been lost, although its adoption as a symbol of the Holy Trinity in the Early Medieval period is mirrored by Thor's hammer being used as symbols of the cross. Whatever the meaning behind the symbol, the *triskele* was ubiquitous for several centuries.

This strap slide would have been used to decorate either a harness or possibly a scabbard. Many similar objects have been recovered across the UK, with horse equipment being particularly decorative in the first century BC.

Iron Age representations of the *triskele*. (*Left to right*: ESS-2BB5FA, BH-33103E and YORYM-0E0534)

38. Roman rider figurine (ESS-33D3A2)
Found near Roxwell.
AD 43–410

The horse and rider is a particularly abundant form in Roman Britain, with the most common depictions on brooches. Whether this image was a deity local to Britain, or simply a representation of a Romano-British man riding on a horse, it was clearly a symbol recognised across the province. Often, these symbols had religious connotations; a local deity associated with horses was Epona.

The object below is a male and, from the position of the legs, would have sat atop an animal. There is evidence that the cape would have been attached to something, although no trace of that remains. No similar examples have been found, making this quite an exceptional piece and perhaps evidence of an adaptation of a more widespread design.

A horse and rider brooch from the Isle of Wight (IOW-74EB3E).

39. Roman stone testing piece (ESS-E5CE07)
Found near Roxwell.
AD 350-400

One aspect of the past that is often lacking is production. Most of the material found during excavations or through metal detecting is the finished product, and would have been used in daily life. However, understanding how these objects were produced is much more difficult, and there are often few textual sources that explain how objects were made.

This object is a test piece, used by a jeweller during the Roman period. It is clear that, before attempting to carve the design of an object into a mould, they would practise on pieces of stone such as this to ensure the desired effect would be produced when the object was cast. Just as with coins, it is quite easy to carve the design incorrectly, as it needs to be the reverse of the intended design. Practicing on pieces of stone like this improves the chances of an accurate casting of the final object.

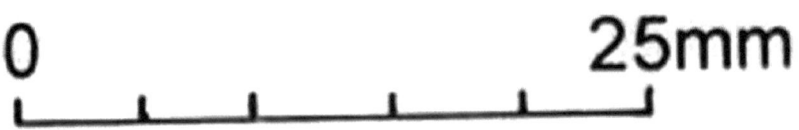

0   25mm

76

40. Early Medieval horned mount (ESS-D6ACD5)
Found in Chelmsford district.
AD 750–800

In the Early Medieval period, animals are often depicted on objects, although it is not always possible to tell what species they were meant to be. 'Beasts', as they are often referred to, can be seen on a variety of metal objects throughout the period and are included on both Anglo-Saxon and Viking objects.

This mount appears to depict a bull, or some other horned creature. The features on the face are quite stylised, making it difficult to tell for certain what species this is meant to represent. Furthermore, horns are not necessarily exclusive to animals. Woden, god of warfare, was often depicted with horns. Thus it may be possible that this object is actually associated with him, rather than with the more mundane bull.

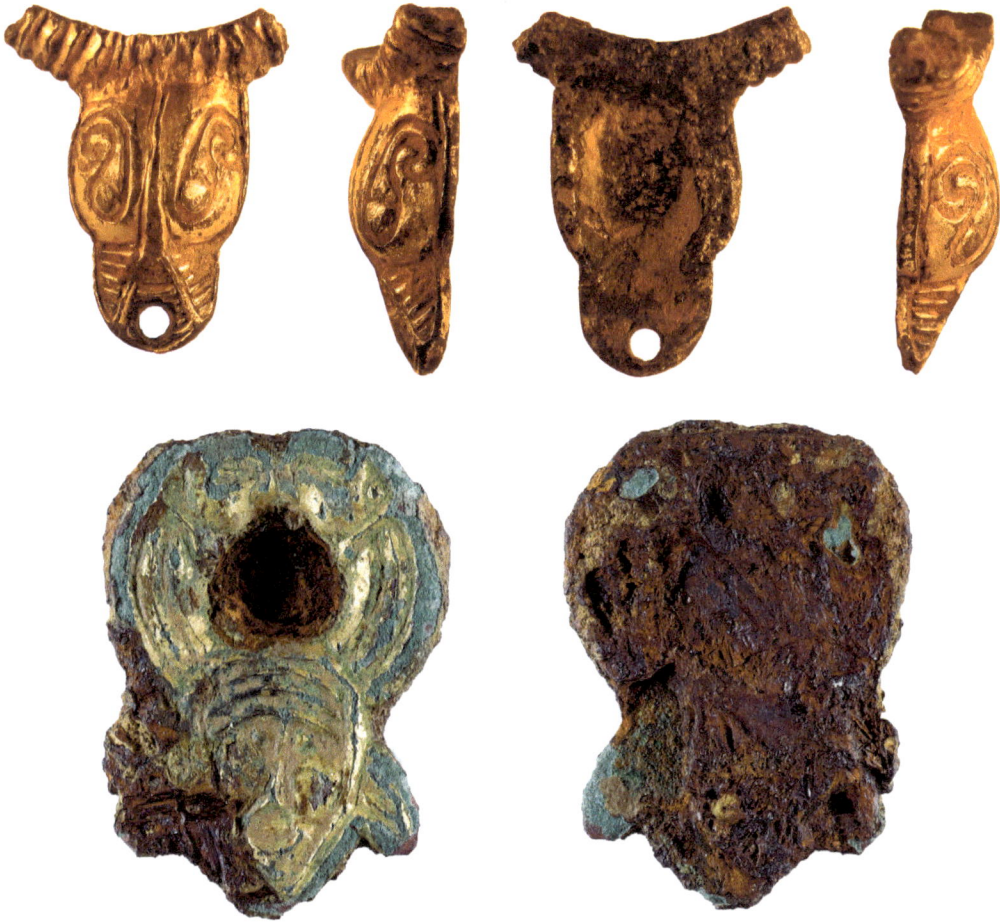

A mount depicting Woden (YORYM-FAE4AF).

41. Medieval 'Romanesque' stylus (ESS-0CEFC4)
Found near Pleshey.
AD 1100–1200

In the Medieval period, objects were regularly decorated with scenes of nature, such as vines and flowers. These designs were often quite stylised and became known collectively as 'Romanesque'.

This object is believed to be from the end of a stylus (a pen used to write on wax), although due to its condition it is difficult to know for certain what the original object was. However, the Romanesque style is clear and the object can be dated to the twelfth century AD, when the style really began to take off. The head is possibly representative of an animal of some sort, although again that is difficult to know for certain.

Chapter 7
Southend, Maldon, Rochford and Castle Point

The south-east of the county is rich in maritime history, but there is much more than just ships and trade. The region has been inhabited throughout history and was once connected to Europe by the landmass known as 'doggerland'. Since the earliest humans inhabited this part of Britain, there has been a great variety of people living in these coastal and estuarine zones.

Today, a large part of this region is owned by the Ministry of Defence and is out of access for most people. This means that metal-detecting is not permitted on a large stretch of the south Essex coast. Despite this, there have been a great many objects found in the fields of this region, each of which provides insight into the history of this part of the county.

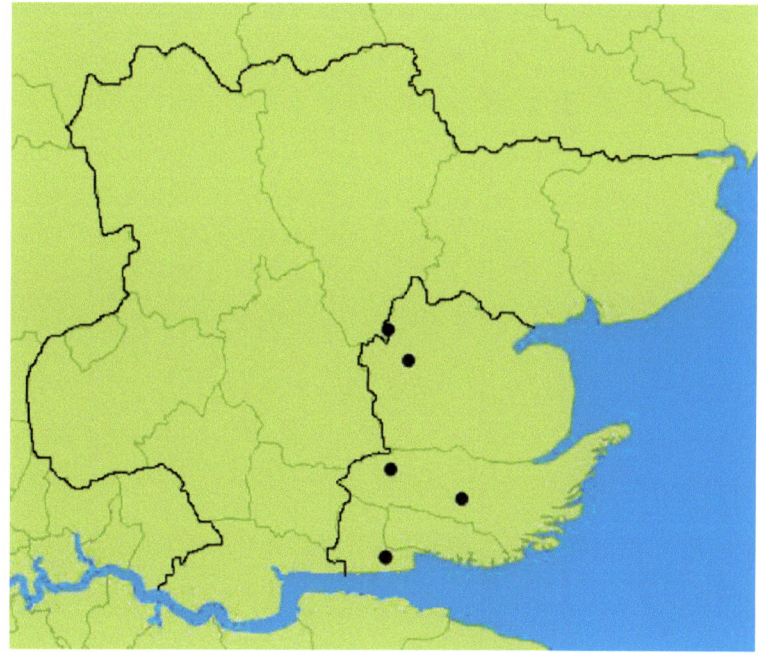

A map of Maldon, Castle Point and Rochford districts and Southend Unitary Authority. (Ben Paites)

42. The Burnham-on-Crouch Hoard (ESS-CC3994)
Found near Burnham-on-Crouch.
1000–800 BC

A defining feature of the late Bronze Age is the presence of metalworking hoards deposited across the country. These hoards consist of a variety of objects, although socketed axes are by far the most common find. What sets these hoards apart is the presence of objects that seem to have been intentionally broken.

The Burnham-on-Crouch hoard is quite typical of the hoards of this period, although exceptional in its size. It contained 214 objects, including socketed axes, palstaves, swords and a large amount of metalworking waste. One interesting fragment is part of a sword that would have come all the way from central Europe. In the earliest form of recycling, it is believed Bronze Age metalworkers often deposited large quantities of unfinished or damaged bronze objects to be melted down and recast into new objects.

The handle of a *volgriffschwert* (full-grip sword) from Central Europe (ESS-3CD836).

Part of the Burnham-on-Crouch hoard being excavated in the lab. (Portable Antiquities Scheme)

43. Roman votive axe (ESS-B42710)
Found on Canvey Island.
AD 43–410

Throughout history, humans have worshipped in nature and provided offerings to the gods. In the Roman period, these offerings could sometimes be personal items, but often they were highly symbolic of the thing they were asking the gods to do. This has meant that miniature objects have been found associated with religious sites across the country.

This miniature axe may have been made as an offering to the gods. Vulcan is one god associated with tools, so perhaps this was an offering made to him by a metalworker in an attempt to ensure good business. The variety of miniature objects found and recorded with the PAS highlights the range of demands people living in Roman Britain had for the gods.

A Roman plate brooch in the form of an axe, found in Dorset (DOR-8F9551).

44. Roman jet hairpin depicting a human face (ESS-C03955)
Found on Canvey Island.
AD 43–410

The style in which you wore your hair in the Roman world was a regularly changing and incredibly important part of social life. For women in particular, fashionable hairstyles changed regularly, as can be seen in coinage throughout the Roman Empire. In order to achieve such elaborate and sometimes outlandish hairstyles, it was important to have the correct accessories. Often, the objects used to create these hairstyles were just as ostentatious as the hair themselves.

This pin was made in the second century and is formed of jet. There is one known source of jet that would have been available at this time in the UK and that is in Whitby. The pin appears to have a face carved into the top and is highly stylised. The material indicates that the owner may have been wealthy, while the style of decoration points to indigenous British production. Most hairpins from this period were made of bone or more rarely bronze, but the few jet examples that have been found hint at luxury.

Radiate of Julia Domna showing a hairstyle typical of the time, AD 196–211 (SF-65C22A).

45. Early Medieval engraved bone knife handle (ESS-CE8616)
Found on Canvey Island.
AD 870–1000

The intricate designs used by the people of Anglo-Saxon England went far beyond their metalwork. There have been examples of engraved objects found across the Anglo-Saxon world, with many highlighting the skill of these craftspeople.

This handle would have been fitted to a knife, probably used daily, for a range of activities including eating and carving. The design is very similar to the knotwork seen on some metalwork already mentioned in this book. This clearly shows that same sorts of designs were used on a variety of different objects of everyday life.

A late Saxon stirrup-strap mount with knotwork design (SUR-7F8074).

46. Medieval staff terminal (SUSS-3C8EA4)
Found near Wickham Bishops.
AD 1000–1300

In the Medieval period, the monarchy and the Church used displays of power as a way of asserting dominance over all those beneath them. This was done through ceremonial actions and the use of objects, such as the crown or mitre, to symbolise their power.

This is a copper alloy sceptre terminal; it is relatively plain for such an object. There were many levels to the power structure in the medieval world, so it is likely that this belonged to a lower-ranking individual. Its discovery near a church would also indicate that it belonged to a member of the clergy rather than the nobility. It has been suggested that the openwork design may indicate it was from an *aspergillum* (holy water dispenser), again suggesting an ecclesiastical origin.

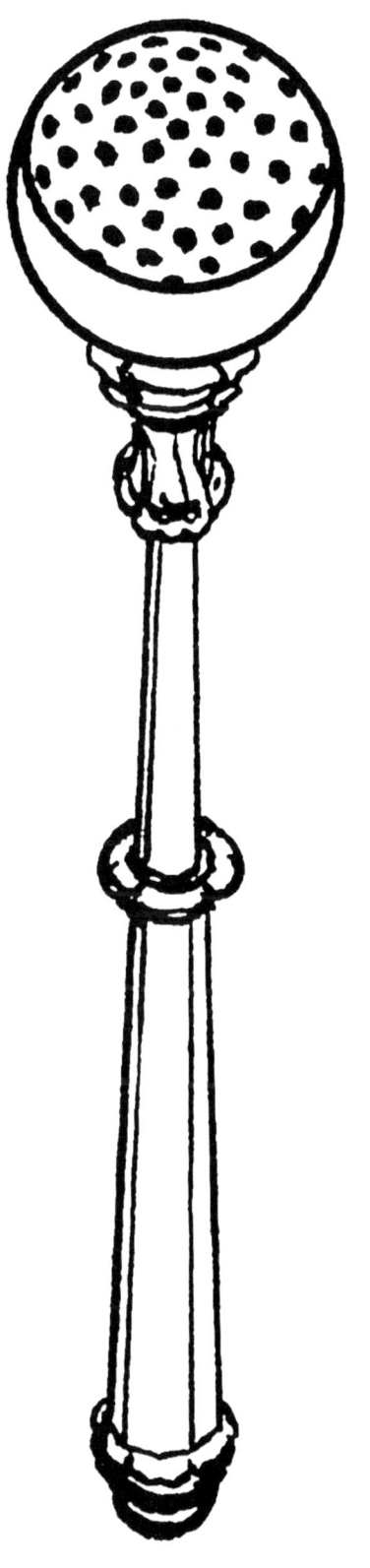

A line drawing of a modern *aspergillum*. (Pearson Scott Foresman)

47. Post-Medieval knife cap in the form of a dog's head (LON-3C6C02)
Found near Maldon.
AD 1500–1600

In the medieval period, hunting was observed by all members of society, but gradually the nobility adopted hunting as a formal pastime. This led to the development in the sixteenth century of large parks that were used exclusively by the elite to keep deer and other animals for regular hunts.

This object would have been the cap on the end of a relatively large knife, believed to have been used for hunting. The form it takes is believed to be that of a spaniel, or similar species of dog. It has been suggested that the spaniel, which was associated with the Talbot family from the earldom of Shrewsbury, could indicate a noble owner. Spaniels were also regularly used in hunting, so this might be a representation of the owner's hunting dog of choice.

An engraving of a wolf-hunt with hounds, dating to the fifteenth century.

48. The Hockley pendant (ESS-2C4836)
Found near Hockley.
AD 1500–1550

The pilgrimage has already been mentioned as an important part of any medieval Christian's life, with shrines selling souvenirs across the Christian world. As well as being a sign of your devotion, some souvenirs were made sacred by containing holy relics. These reliquaries were produced in large quantities, with many claiming to contain fragments of objects associated with the saint or even parts of the deceased saint's body.

This particular reliquary contained fragments of flax, perhaps from a garment worn by the saint in question. The design shows the wounds of Christ on one side and Christ carrying the cross on the other, suggesting the fragment within was associated with Him. The names of the three Magi – Jaspar, Balthazar and Melchior – are written around the edge. Their names were commonly inscribed on objects from this period as a form of spiritual protection. The fact that this object is so ornate and that it is made of gold would suggest it belonged to someone of significant wealth and status. At the same time, it would have been a deeply personal object that reflected the long journey they would have made to get it.

49. Post-Medieval seal matrix depicting a ship (ESS-ED25B6)
Found near Barling Magna.
AD 1500–1700

Having one of the longest coastlines of any county in the UK, maritime history has played a major role in the formation of Essex. After the discovery of the New World in the fifteenth century, large quantities of ships would have sailed through the Thames estuary to reach London, stopping regularly at places along the Essex coast. Therefore, ships would have been a regular site for the people living in this region.

This seal, which features a ship, would have likely been used by a merchant sailor to mark any official documents used in trade and commerce. This type of seal was common throughout the seventeenth and eighteenth centuries, although the style of the ship might suggest an earlier date. Without an inscription it is impossible to link the seal to any individual, but its discovery close to the Thames estuary enforces the notion it belonged to someone involved in maritime trade.

A scene from an eighteenth-century trinket box, showing an inn with sails in the background, suggesting the people may be merchant sailors. (ESS-C819ED)

Chapter 8
Modern Deposition

50. Hindu Ritual Vessels, September 2016
Found in the River Colne.
Not recorded with the PAS

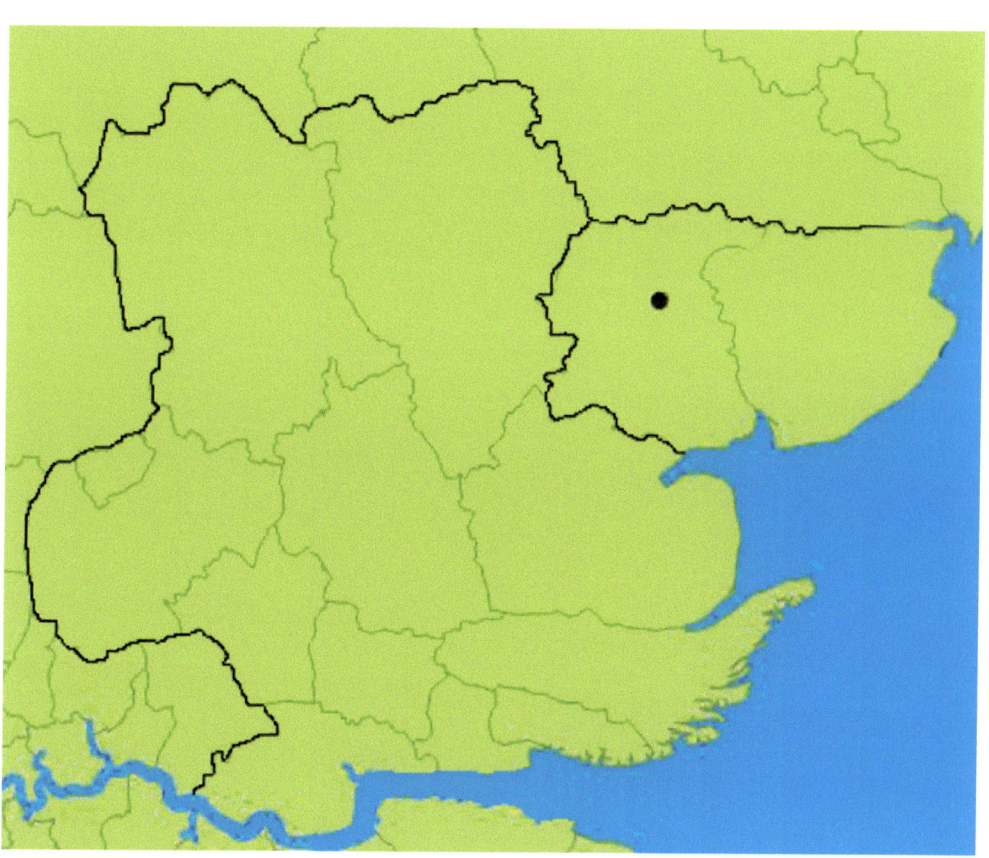

Not all discoveries made in Essex are of ancient objects. In fact, some discoveries of more recent finds can be just as interesting and significant as the discovery of a Roman figurine or Viking sword.

In the summer of 2015, I received a phone call about some ceramic vessels that had been spotted lying at the bottom of the river Colne in Castle Park in Colchester. I went to investigate, along with the conservation officer and a volunteer with the PAS. Having borrowed an extendable arm from the park ranger, we managed to retrieve the items and bring them back to the museum for cleaning. Having seen similar objects previously in London, it became clear to me that these vessels had been used in a Hindu ritual before being deposited in the water.

After getting in contact with the Sri Ram temple in Clacton-on-Sea, I was invited to bring the objects to be examined. It soon became clear that these vessels were related to a funerary ritual and had been placed in the river as an offering for the deceased to have a safe journey into the afterlife. Though traditionally constructed using biodegradable material, such as leaves of unbaked clay, the intention behind the action was clear. Realising the religious significance, the objects were ritually cleansed and have subsequently become part of Colchester Museums' collections.

This is the first documented case of such a practice occurring in Colchester. These customs have been observed in London, where a large Hindu population has been present for many years, but the evidence of this in Colchester clearly highlights the cultural diversification occurring in the town. These vessels show that changes that still occur within society today and objects continue to be deposited, whether in the ground or in rivers, for future archaeologists to uncover. The recovery of these vessels, and their documentation and storage with Colchester museums, means that future generations will benefit from knowing the exact circumstances surrounding the first ritual deposition relating to Hindu culture in the town.